The flying

Story by Annette Smi...

Illustrated by Xiangyi Mo and Jingwen Wang

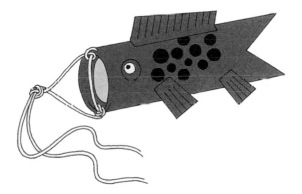

"It's Kite Day on Sunday," said Alex.
"Are you coming, Jonathan?
I'm getting a new kite.
My Dad's going to buy it for me."

"I haven't got a kite,"
said Jonathan.
He walked home slowly.

"Dad," said Jonathan,
"can you buy me a kite
to take to the park on Sunday?
Alex is going.
He is taking his new kite."

Dad smiled at Jonathan.
"I can **make** kites," he said.

"Come and look at this book,"
said Dad. "Here's a good kite."

"Yes!" said Jonathan.
"It looks like a fish.
Can we make that one?"

He went to get some paper.

Jonathan and Dad made the kite.

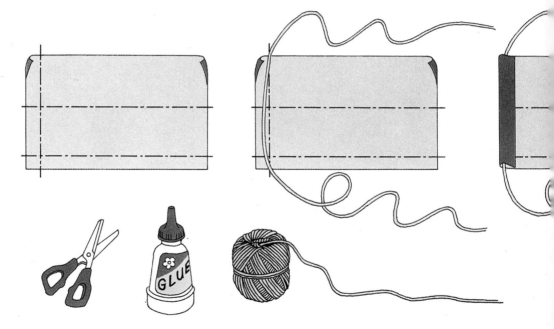

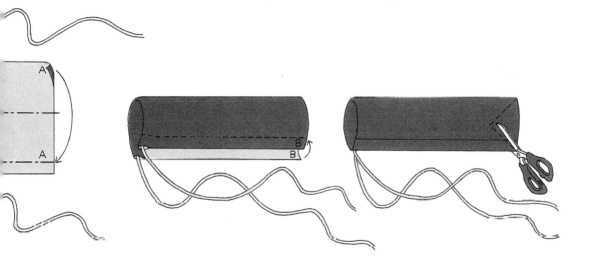

Jonathan cut out the tail.
Then he made some fins,
and some round spots
and two big eyes.

"My kite **looks** like a fish now,"
said Jonathan,
"and it can open its mouth!"

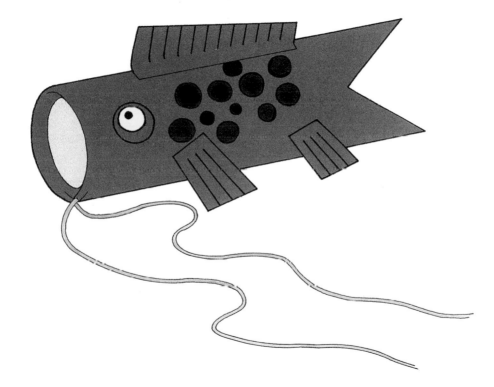

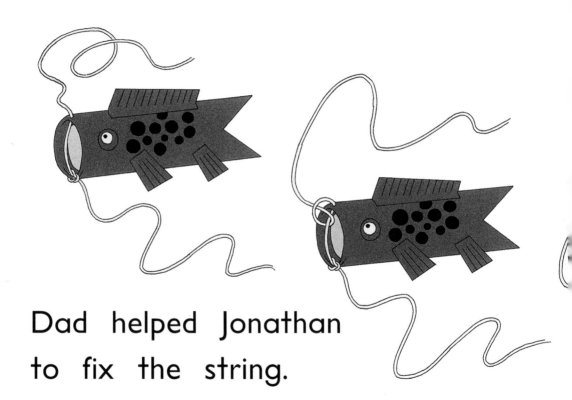

Dad helped Jonathan
to fix the string.

Then they tied the string
to a long stick.

On Kite Day, Jonathan and Dad walked over to the park.
Alex saw Jonathan.
"I like your kite," Alex said.
"It looks like a fish."

"It's a **flying** fish," said Jonathan.
"My Dad helped me make it."

"Come on," said Alex.
"Let's fly our kites."